ED EMBERLEY'S BIG RED DRAWING BOOK

ED EMBERLEY'S BIG RED DRAWING BOOK

LITTLE, BROWN AND COMPANY / BOSTON TORONTO

*FIRST EDITION

LIBRARY OF CONGRESS
CATALOGING-IN-PUBLICATION DATA

EMBERLEY, ED.
ED EMBERLEY'S BIG RED DRAWING BOOK

SUMMARY: PRESENTS STEP-BY-STEP INSTRUCTIONS
FOR DRAWING PEOPLE, ANIMALS AND OBJECTS
USING A MINIMUM OF LINE AND CIRCLE COMBINATIONS.
  1. DRAWING--TECHNIQUE--JUVENILE LITERATURE.
[1. DRAWING--TECHNIQUE] I. TITLE. II. TITLE: BIG
RED DRAWING BOOK.

NC730.E64 1987   741.2'6   87-3091
ISBN 0-316-23434-6
ISBN 0-316-23435-4 (PBK.)

HC: 10 9 8 7 6 5 4 3 2
PB: 10 9 8 7 6 5 4 3 2

WOR

PUBLISHED SIMULTANEOUSLY IN CANADA BY
LITTLE, BROWN & COMPANY (CANADA) LIMITED

PRINTED IN THE UNITED STATES OF AMERICA

THIS IS A WRITING ALPHABET.
YOU CAN USE IT TO MAKE WORDS.

ABCDEFGHIJKLMNOPQRSTUVWXYZ

CAT

THIS IS A DRAWING ALPHABET.
YOU CAN USE IT TO MAKE PICTURES.

HERE'S HOW...THIS ROW SHOWS WHAT TO DRAW, THIS ROW SHOWS WHERE TO PUT IT.

THIS SYMBOL MEANS "FILL IN."

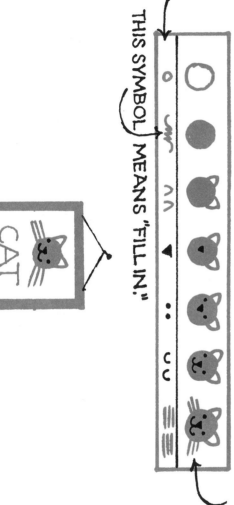

CAT

RED

IS A JUST-RIGHT COLOR FOR DRAWING LOTS OF THINGS, SUCH AS :

RED ANTS, MEASLES, CRANBERRIES, HOLLY BERRIES, CHECKERS,

CHERRY OR STRAWBERRY LOLLIPOPS, JAPANESE FLAGS, RED-CROSS FLAGS, DANGER FLAGS,

CHERRIES,

STRAW-BERRIES,

TOMATOES,

APPLES,

RADISHES,

TULIPS,

ROSES.

PINK

(LIGHT RED) IS A JUST-RIGHT COLOR FOR DRAWING A FEW THINGS

SUCH AS: BUBBLE GUM, CHEEKS, NOSES, STRAWBERRY ICE CREAM,

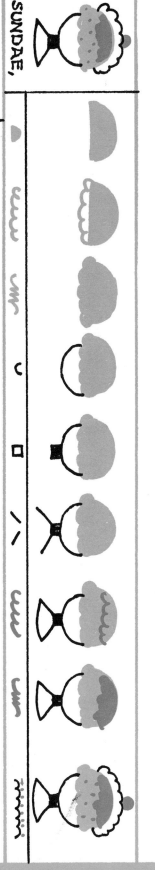

SUNDAE,

WATERMELON,

BUBBLE,

PINK ELEPHANT.

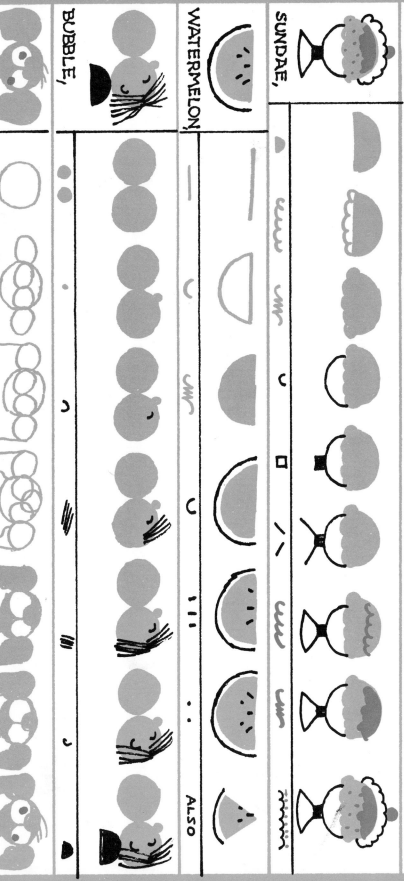

ALSO

RED WHITE AND BLUE

ARE JUST-RIGHT COLORS FOR DRAWING AMERICAN AND OTHER FLAGS AND THINGS SUCH AS:

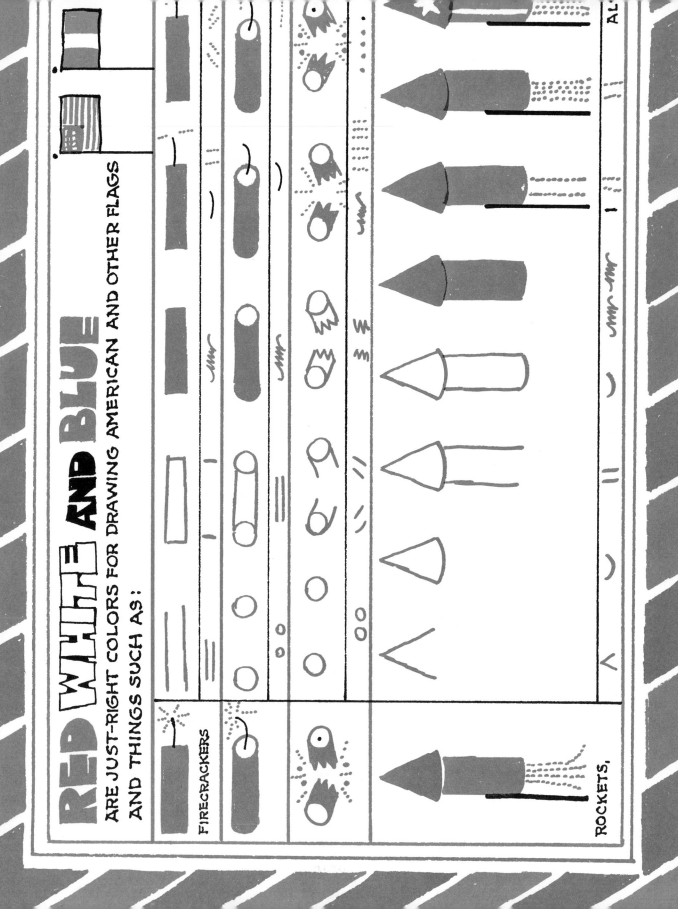

FIRECRACKERS

ROCKETS,

SWAGS, DRAPES, AND BUNTING.

LIBERTY BELL

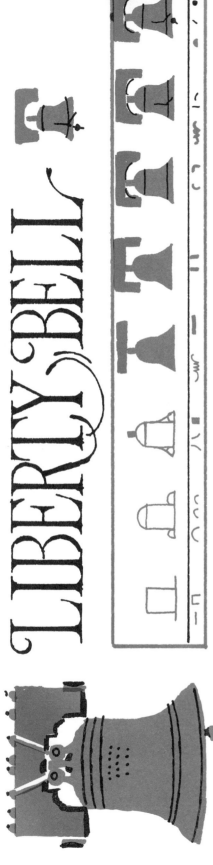

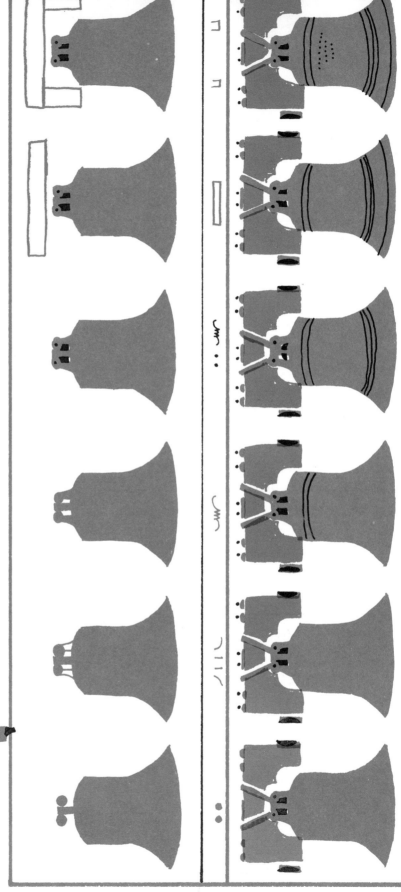

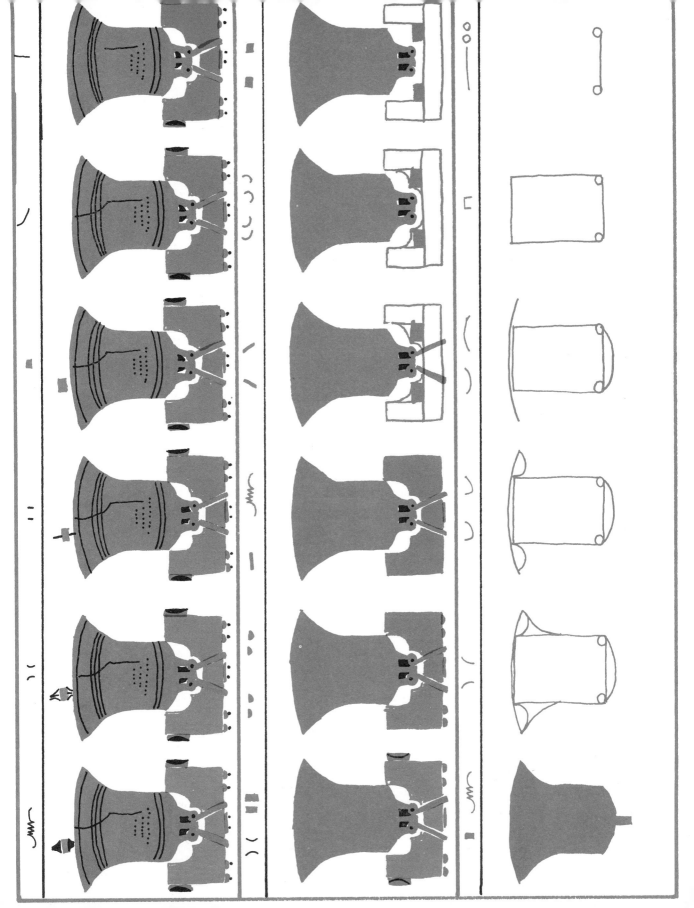

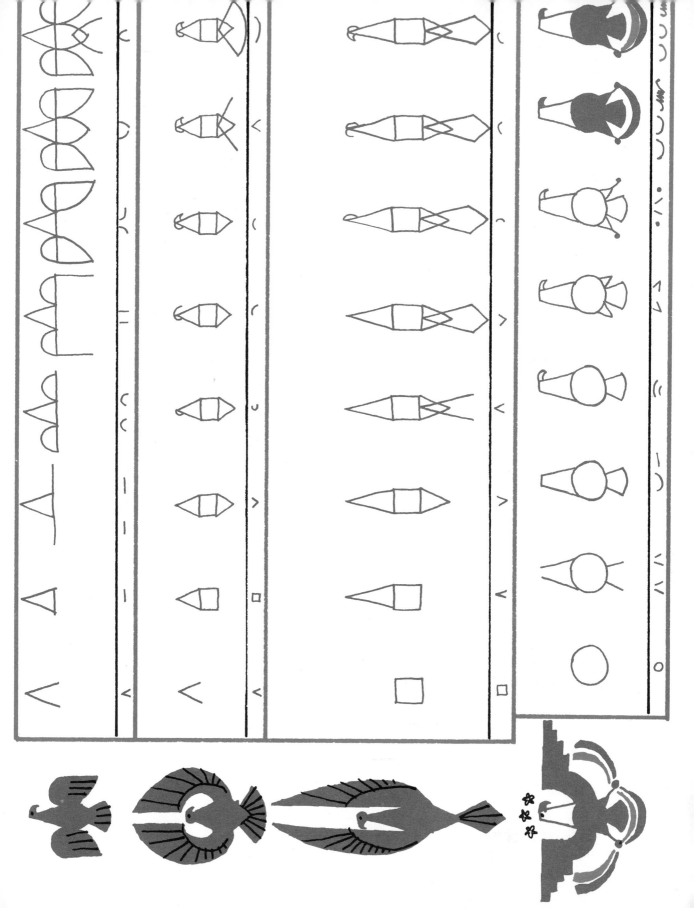

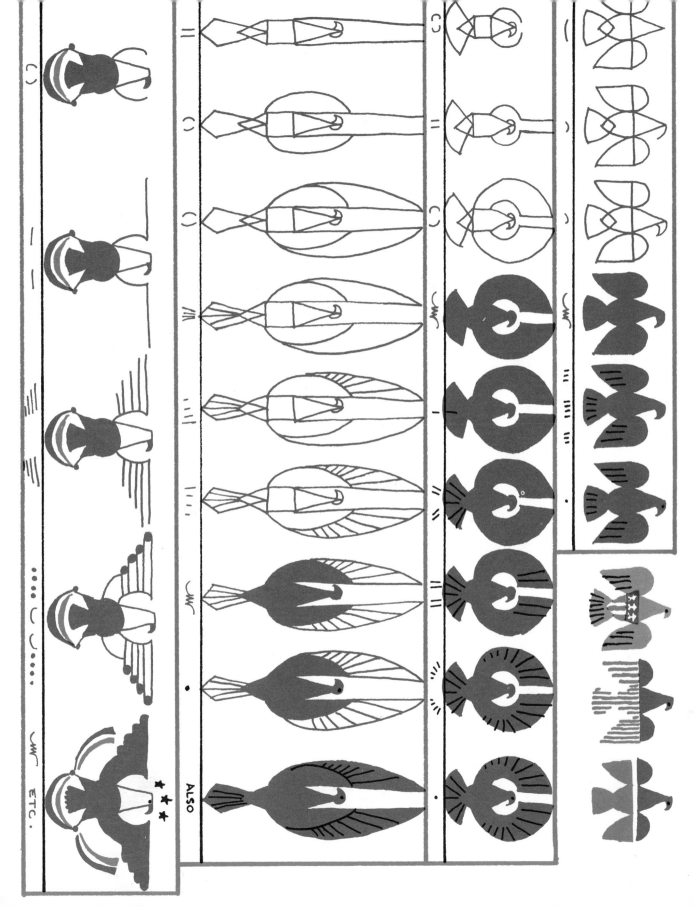

ALSO

ETC.

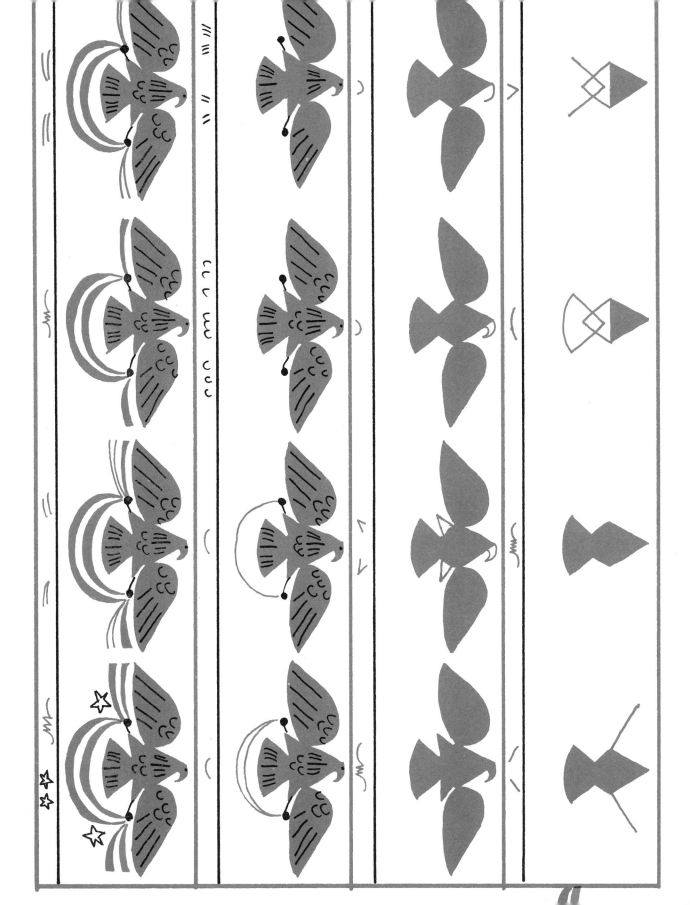

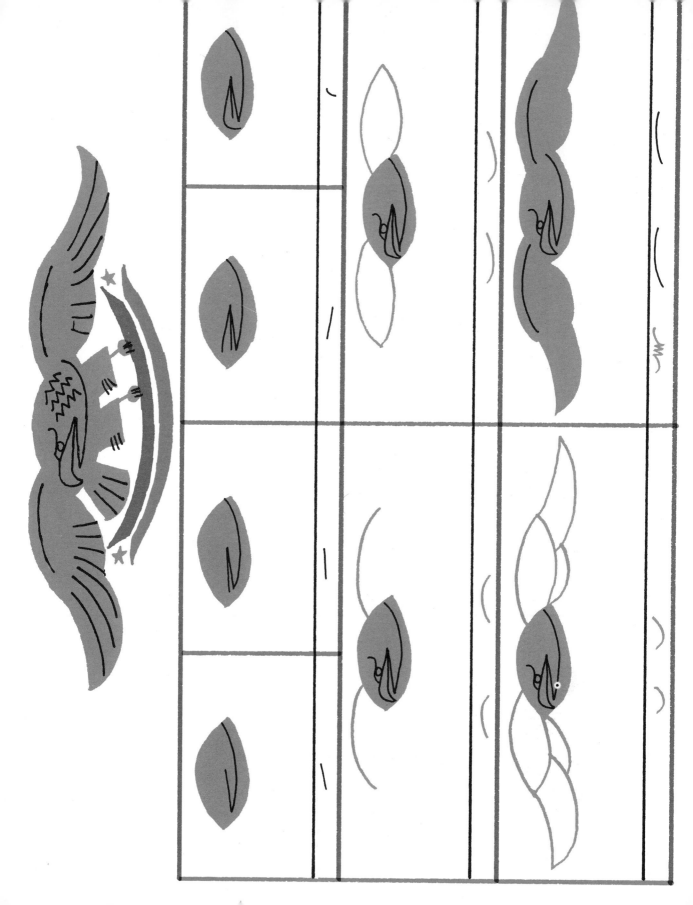

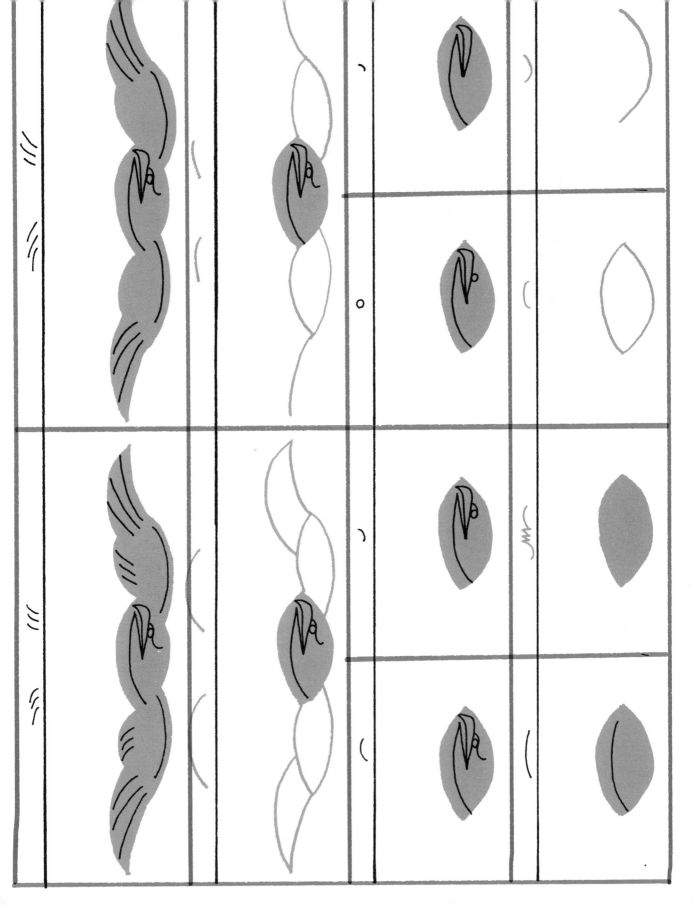

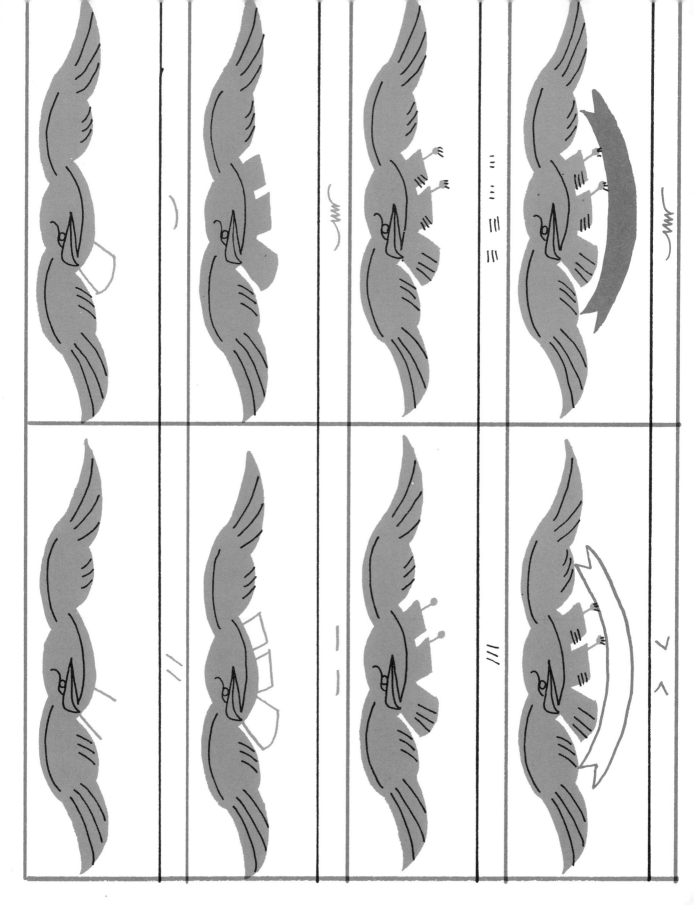

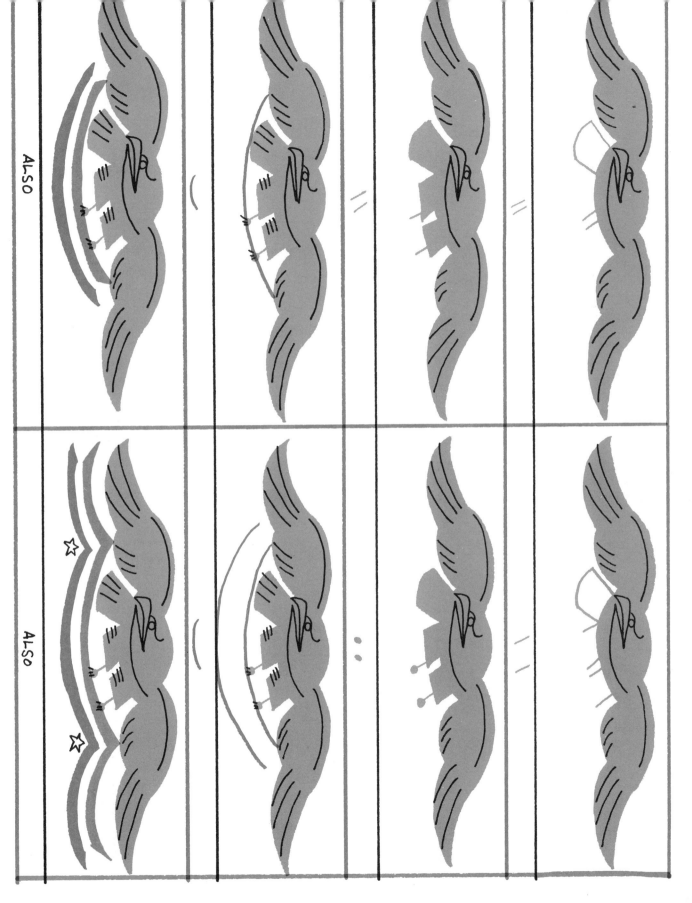

ALSO

ALSO

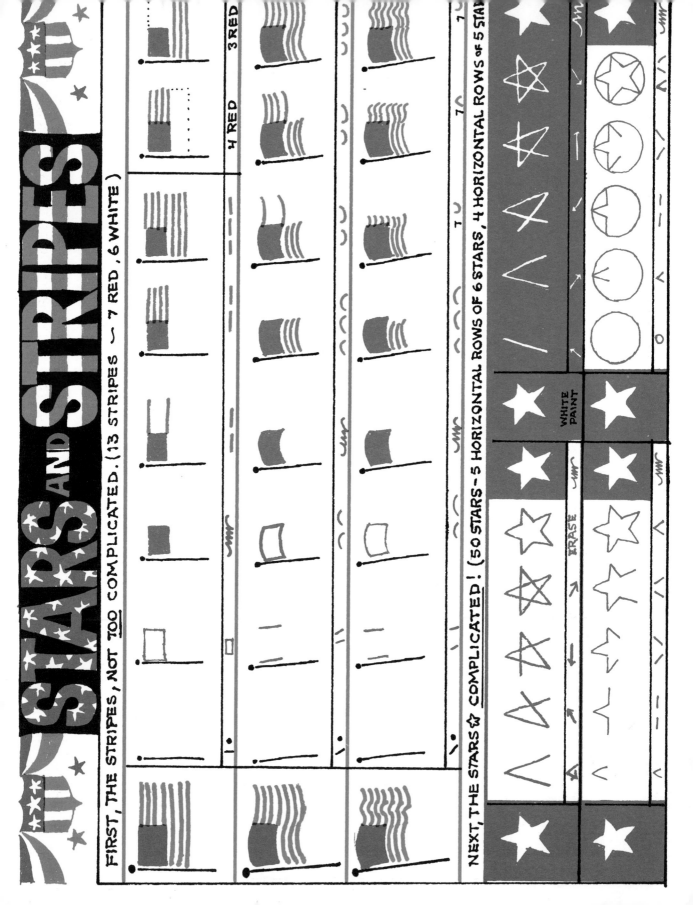

STARS AND STRIPES

FIRST, THE STRIPES, NOT TOO COMPLICATED. (13 STRIPES ~ 7 RED, 6 WHITE)

3 RED
4 RED

NEXT, THE STARS ☆ COMPLICATED! (50 STARS ~ 5 HORIZONTAL ROWS OF 6 STARS, 4 HORIZONTAL ROWS OF 5 STARS)

WHITE PAINT
ERASE

THE CANTON (THE BLUE RECTANGLE WITH ITS FULL SET OF 50 STARS)
FIRST, A SIMPLE METHOD, GOOD FOR DRAWING SMALL AND/OR FARAWAY FLAGS.

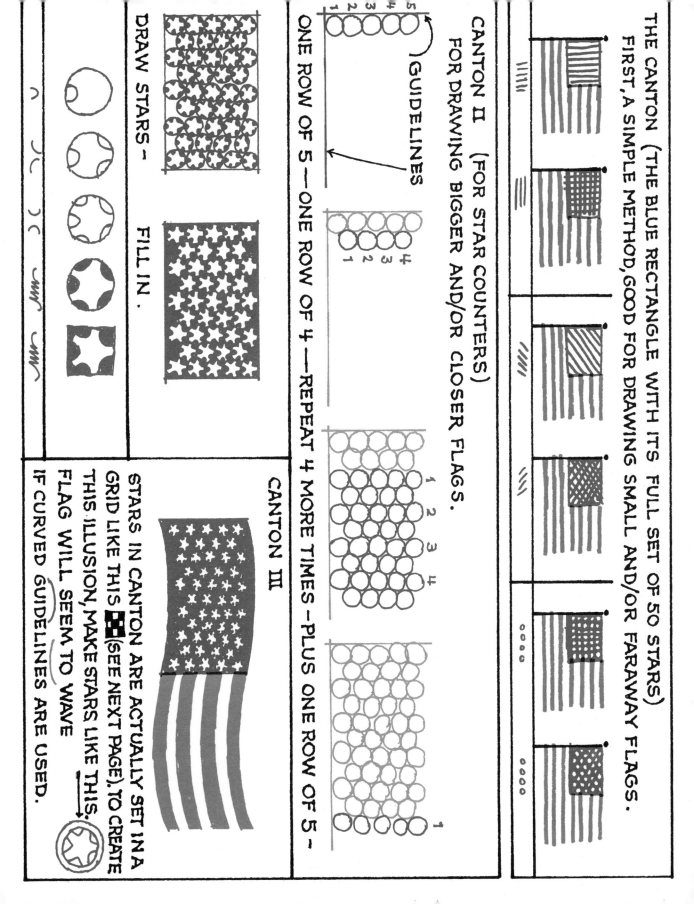

CANTON II (FOR STAR COUNTERS)
FOR DRAWING BIGGER AND/OR CLOSER FLAGS.

GUIDELINES

ONE ROW OF 5—ONE ROW OF 4—REPEAT 4 MORE TIMES—PLUS ONE ROW OF 5—

DRAW STARS~

FILL IN .

CANTON III

STARS IN CANTON ARE ACTUALLY SET IN A GRID LIKE THIS ▓ (SEE NEXT PAGE). TO CREATE THIS ILLUSION, MAKE STARS LIKE THIS. FLAG WILL SEEM TO WAVE IF CURVED GUIDELINES ARE USED.

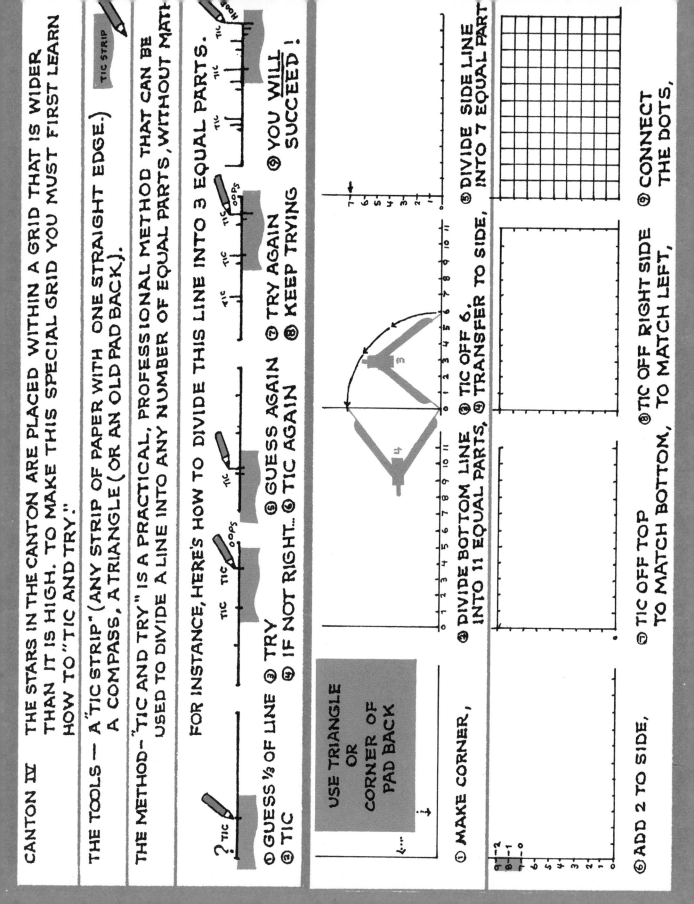

CANTON IV   THE STARS IN THE CANTON ARE PLACED WITHIN A GRID THAT IS WIDER THAN IT IS HIGH. TO MAKE THIS SPECIAL GRID YOU MUST FIRST LEARN HOW TO "TIC AND TRY."

THE TOOLS — A "TIC STRIP" (ANY STRIP OF PAPER WITH ONE STRAIGHT EDGE.) A COMPASS, A TRIANGLE (OR AN OLD PAD BACK).

TIC STRIP

THE METHOD— "TIC AND TRY" IS A PRACTICAL, PROFESSIONAL METHOD THAT CAN BE USED TO DIVIDE A LINE INTO ANY NUMBER OF EQUAL PARTS, WITHOUT MATH.

FOR INSTANCE, HERE'S HOW TO DIVIDE THIS LINE INTO 3 EQUAL PARTS.

① GUESS ⅓ OF LINE   ③ TRY   ⑤ GUESS AGAIN   ⑦ TRY AGAIN   ⑨ YOU WILL
② TIC   ④ IF NOT RIGHT...   ⑥ TIC AGAIN   ⑧ KEEP TRYING   SUCCEED!

USE TRIANGLE OR CORNER OF PAD BACK

① MAKE CORNER,   ② DIVIDE BOTTOM LINE INTO 11 EQUAL PARTS,   ③ TIC OFF 6,   ④ TRANSFER TO SIDE,   ⑤ DIVIDE SIDE LINE INTO 7 EQUAL PARTS

⑥ ADD 2 TO SIDE,   ⑦ TIC OFF TOP TO MATCH BOTTOM,   ⑧ TIC OFF RIGHT SIDE TO MATCH LEFT,   ⑨ CONNECT THE DOTS,

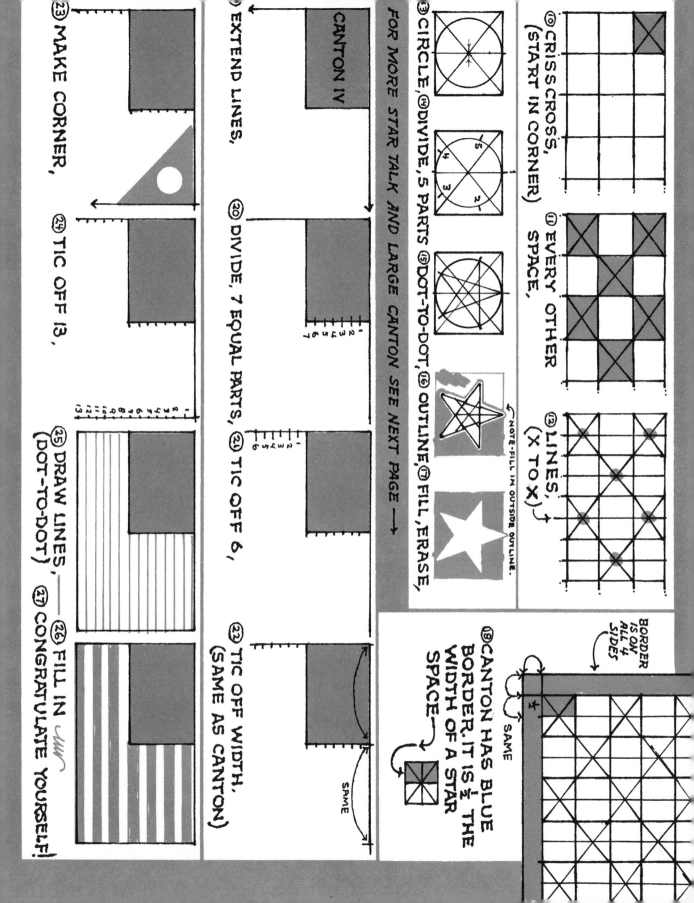

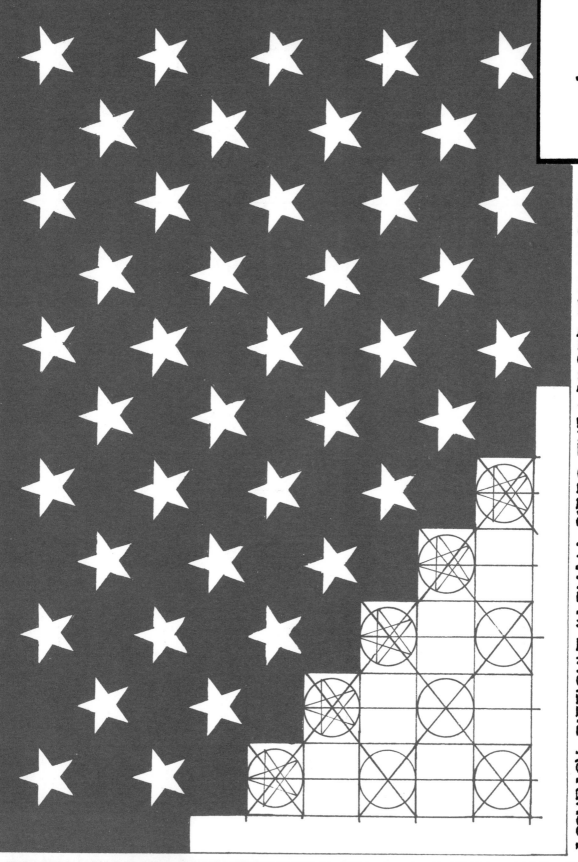

ACCURACY-DIFFICULT IN SMALL SIZES THE LARGER THE EASIER
CANTON Ⅴ-A FURTHER REFINEMENT, STAR POINTS SHOULD TOUCH
TOP AND BOTTOM OF STAR BOX (BUT NOT THE SIDES).

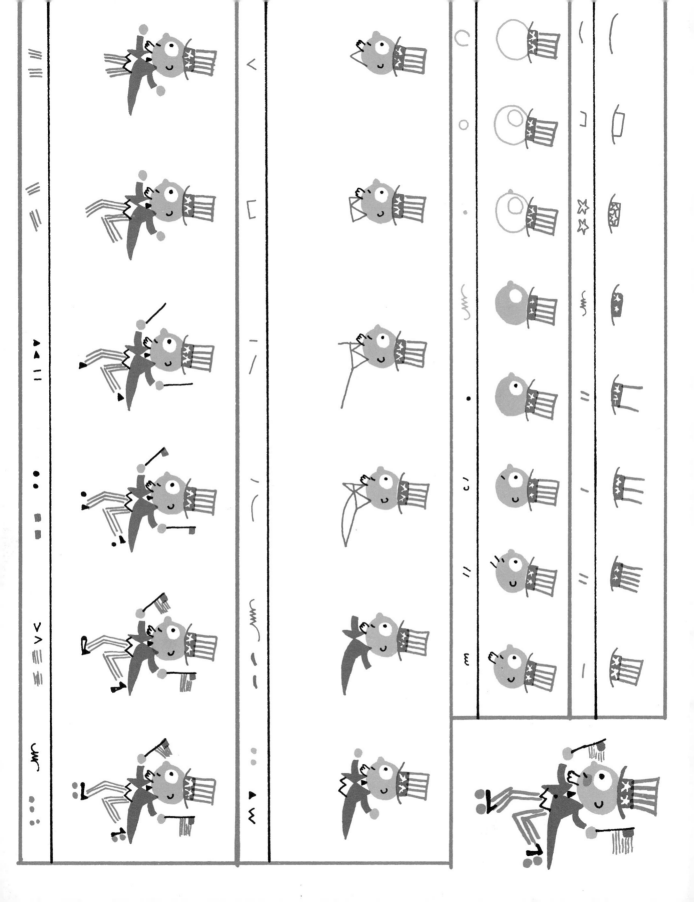

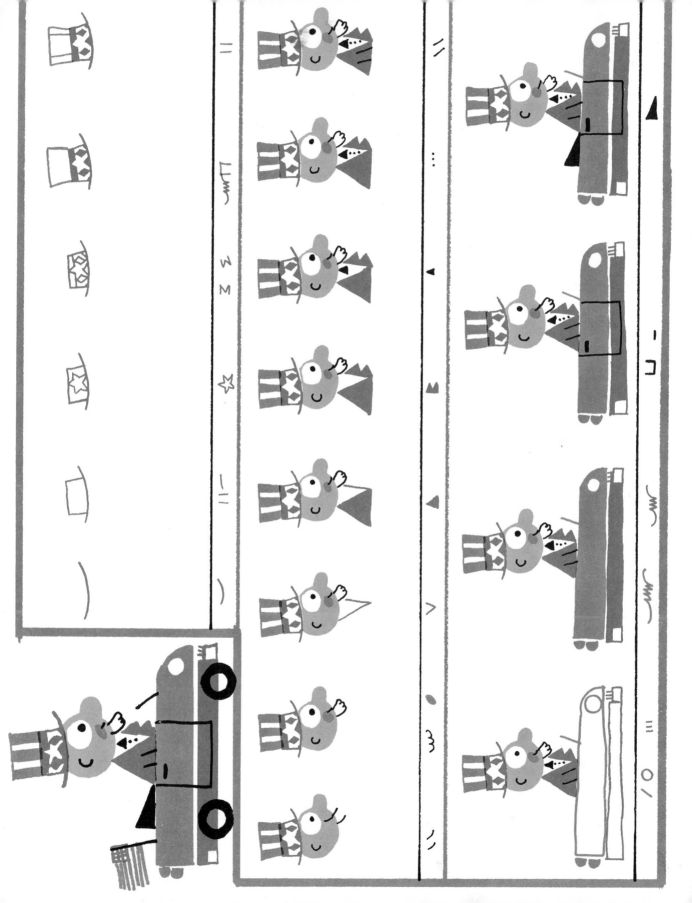

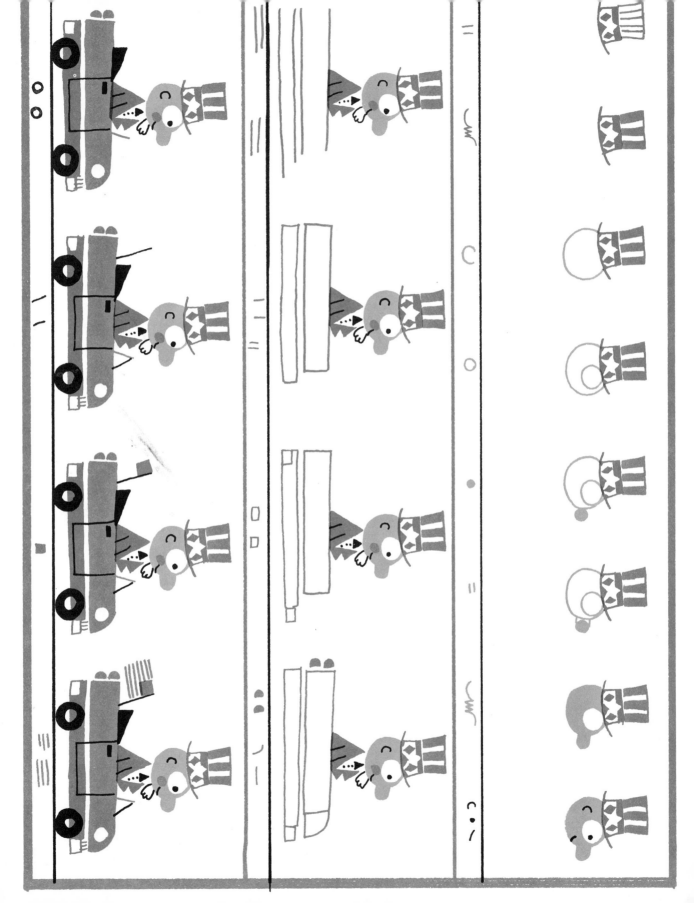

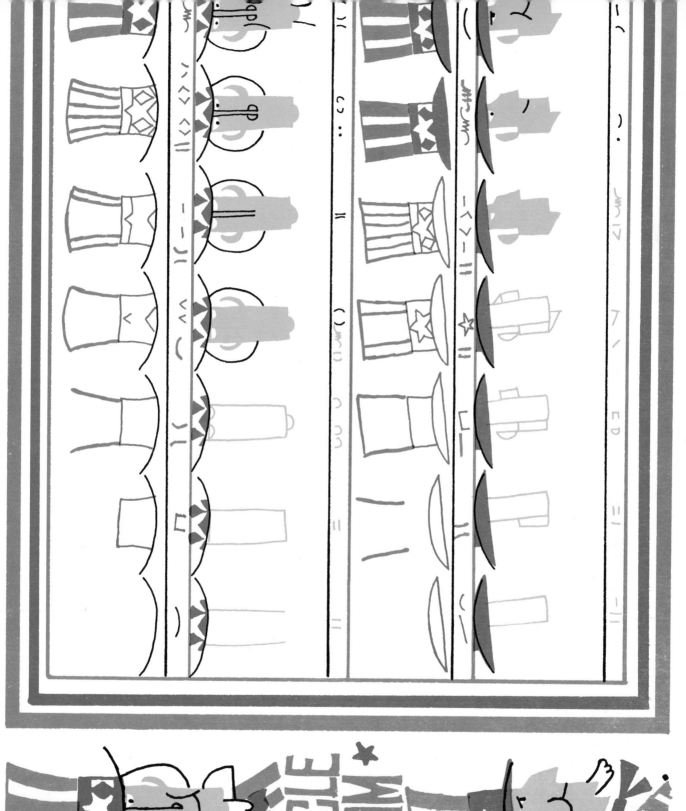

UNCLE
SAM

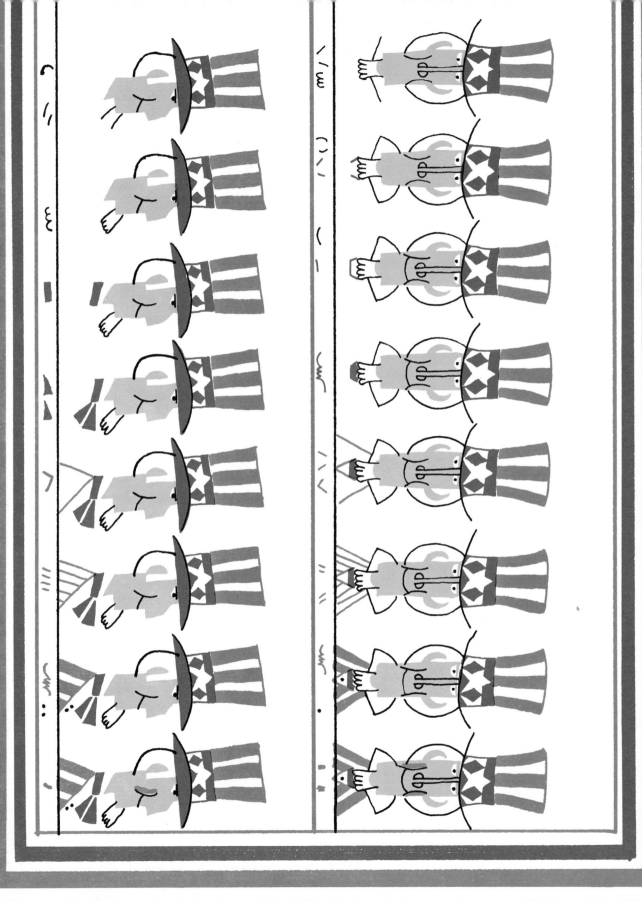

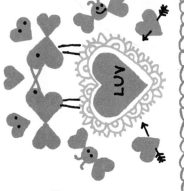

VALENTINE'S DAY

LUV

HOP | WALK | RUNNING | HAPPY HEART

LOVE BUG

LOVE BIRD

VALENTINE

LUV

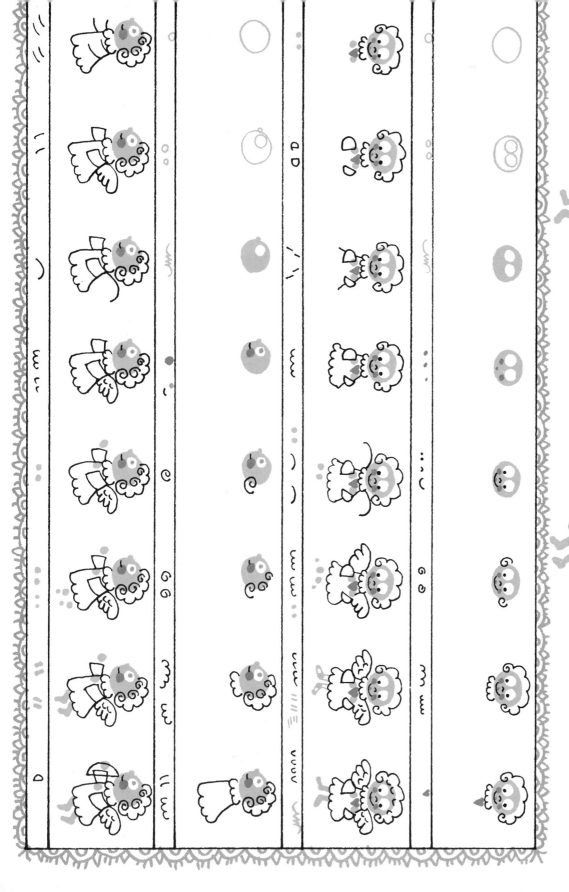

CUPID

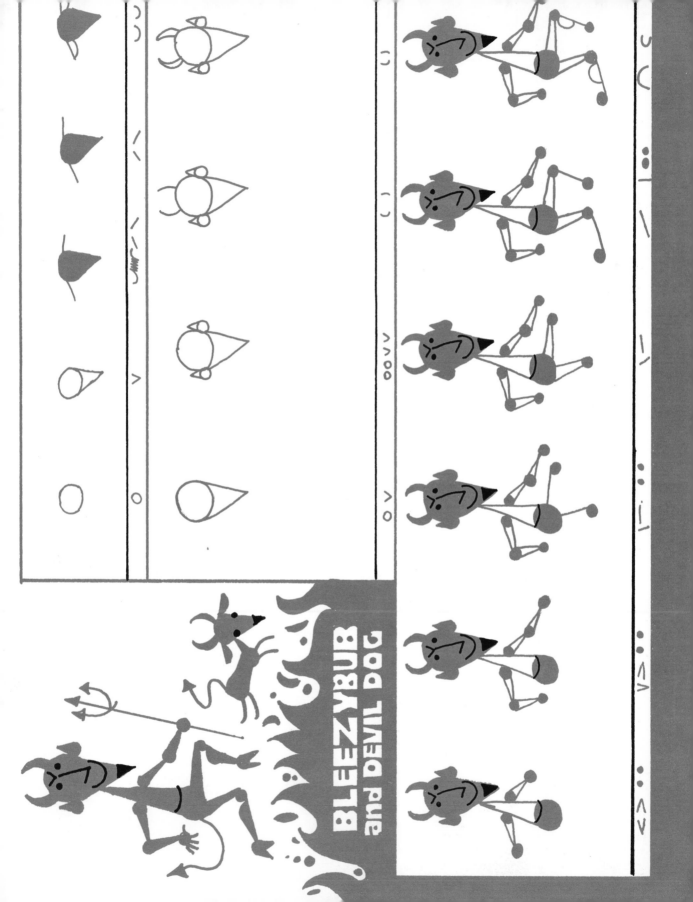

BLEEZYBUB and DEVIL DOG

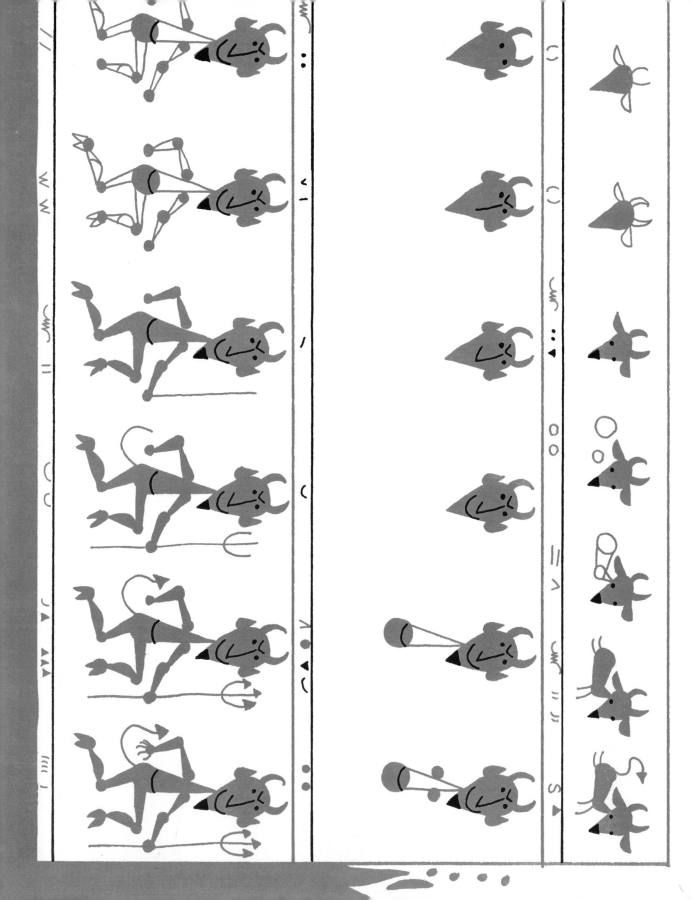

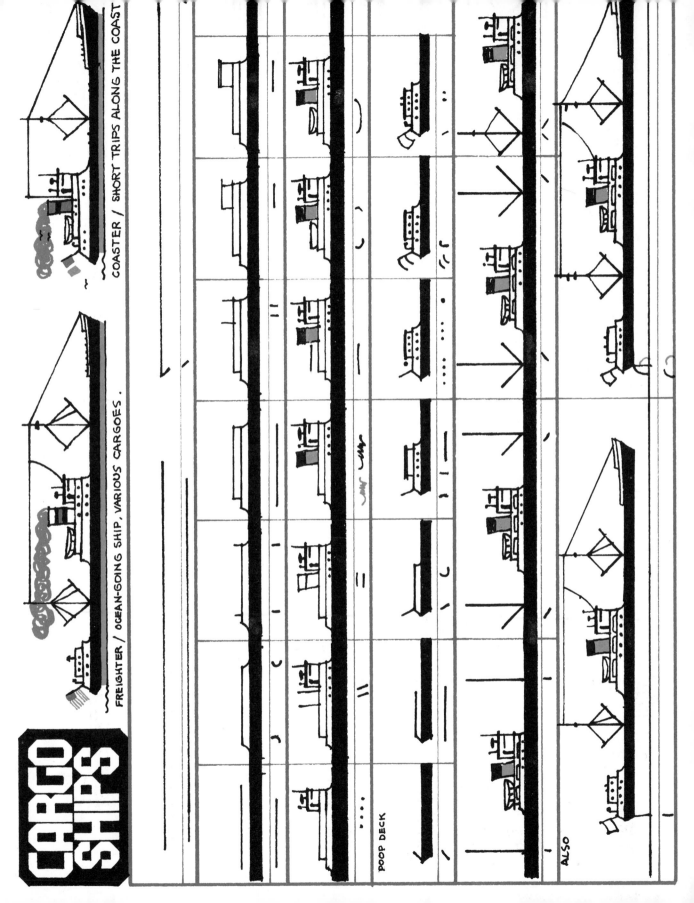

CARGO SHIPS

FREIGHTER / OCEAN-GOING SHIP, VARIOUS CARGOES.

COASTER / SHORT TRIPS ALONG THE COAST

POOP DECK

ALSO

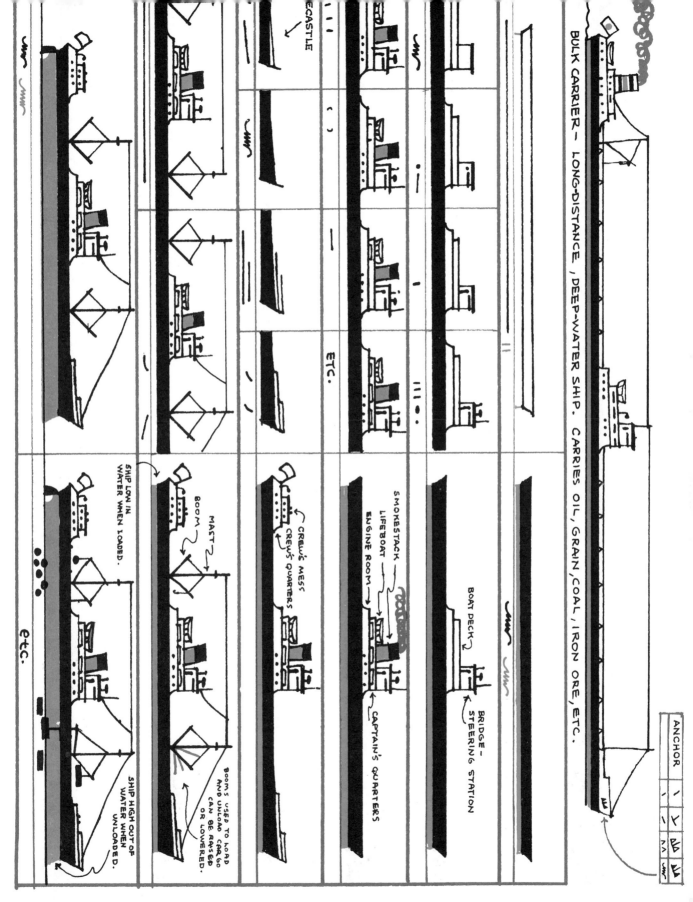

BULK CARRIER — LONG-DISTANCE, DEEP-WATER SHIP. CARRIES OIL, GRAIN, COAL, IRON ORE, ETC.

FORECASTLE

ETC.

etc.

SHIP LOW IN WATER WHEN LOADED.

SHIP HIGH OUT OF WATER WHEN UNLOADED.

BOOM

MAST

BOOMS USED TO LOAD AND UNLOAD CARGO CAN BE RAISED OR LOWERED.

CREW'S MESS

CREW'S QUARTERS

SMOKESTACK

LIFEBOAT

ENGINE ROOM

CAPTAIN'S QUARTERS

BOAT DECK

BRIDGE — STEERING STATION

ANCHOR

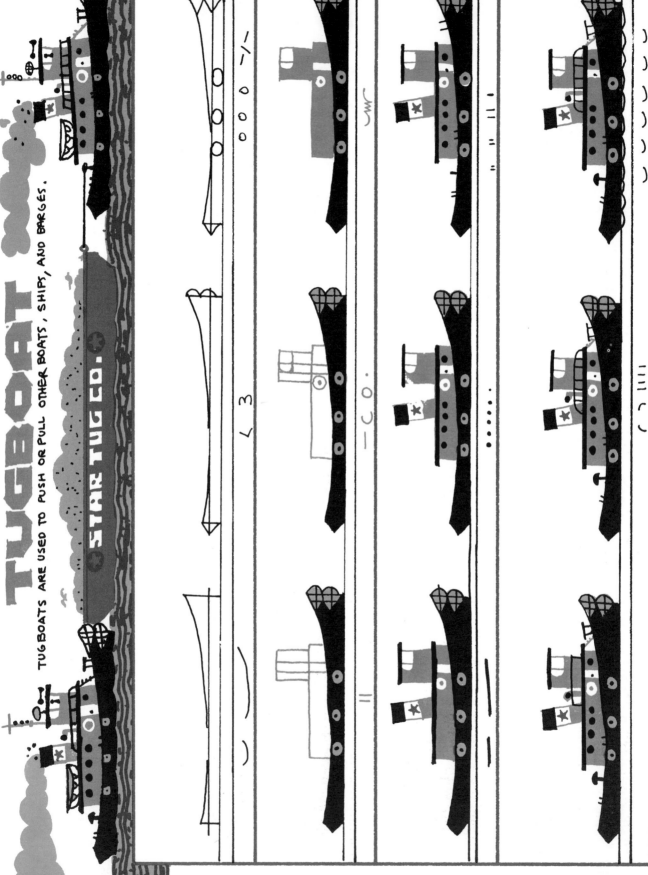

TUGBOAT

TUGBOATS ARE USED TO PUSH OR PULL OTHER BOATS, SHIPS, AND BARGES.

STAR TUG CO.

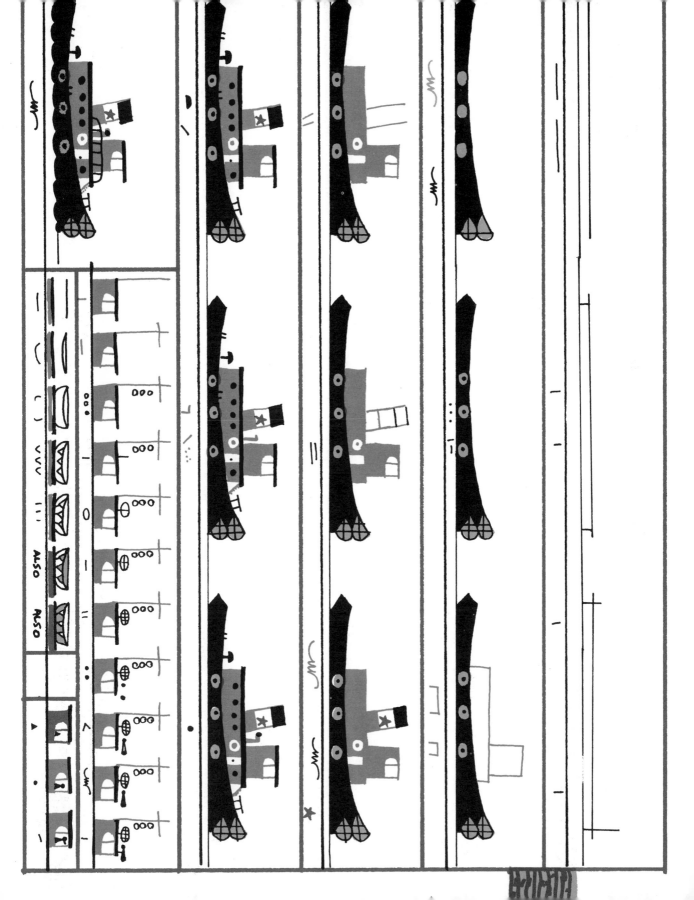

LIGHTSHIP

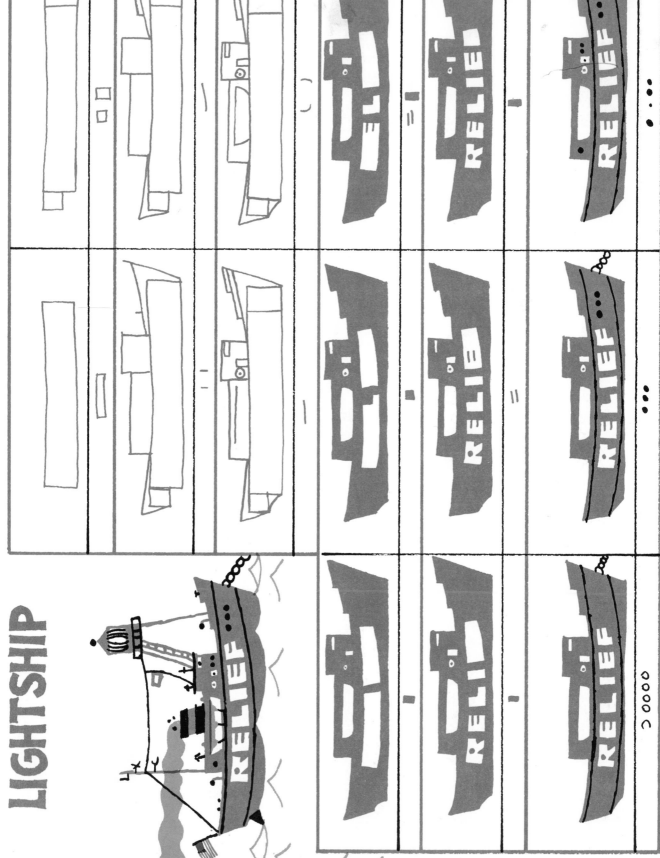

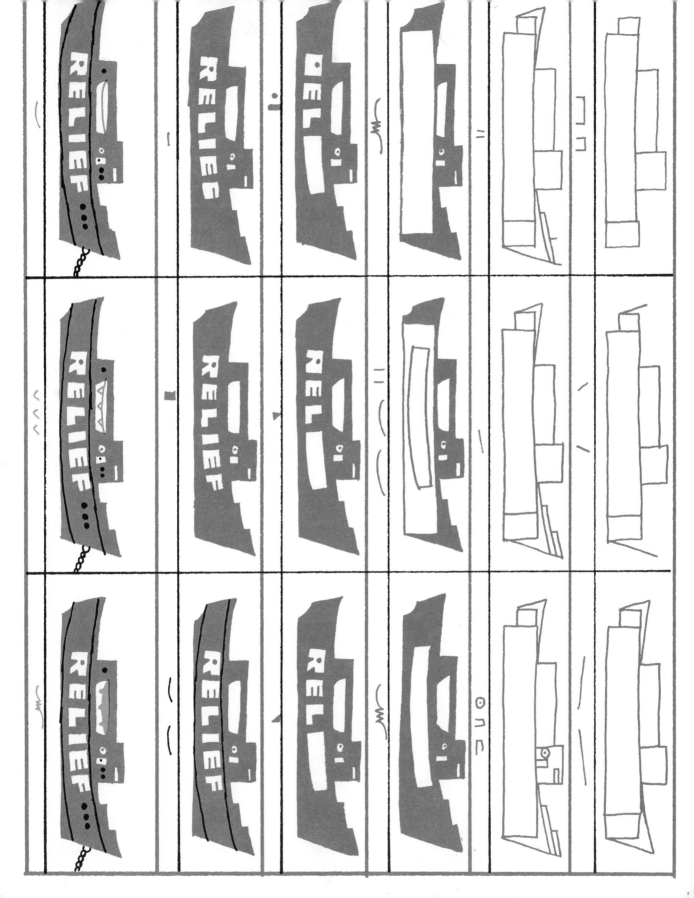

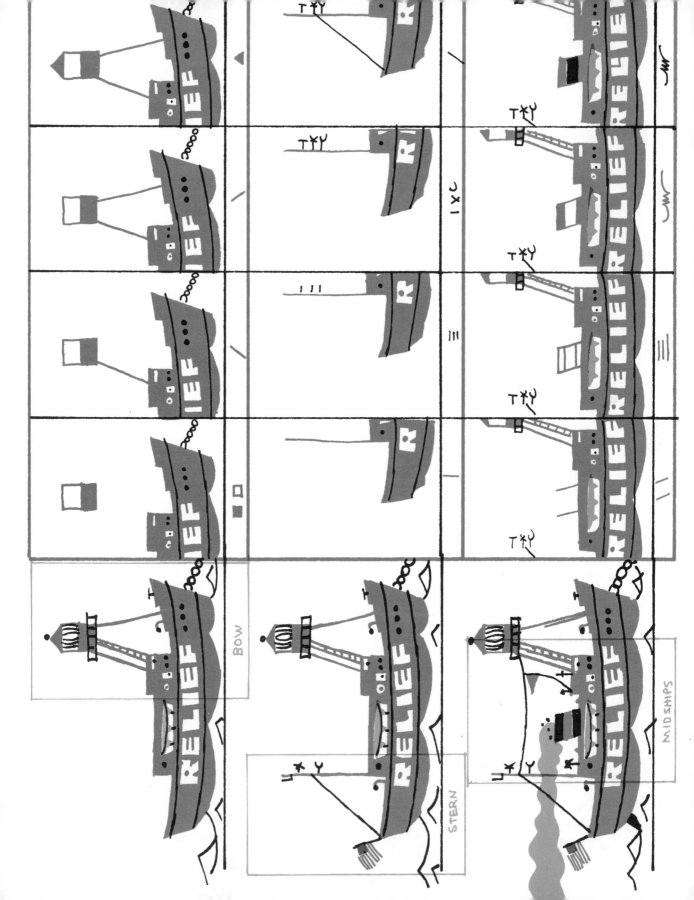

BOW

STERN

MIDSHIPS

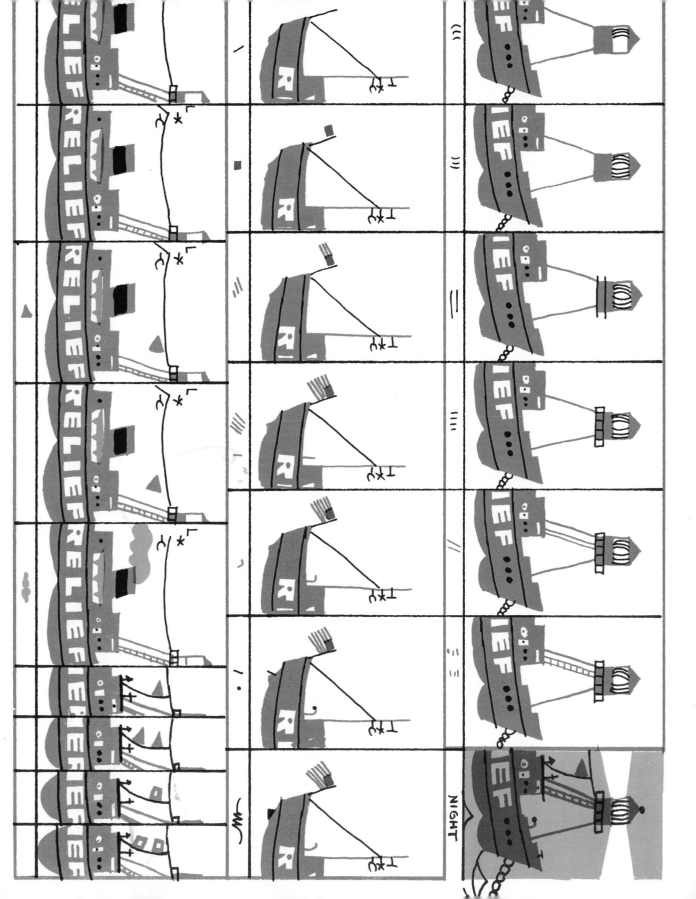

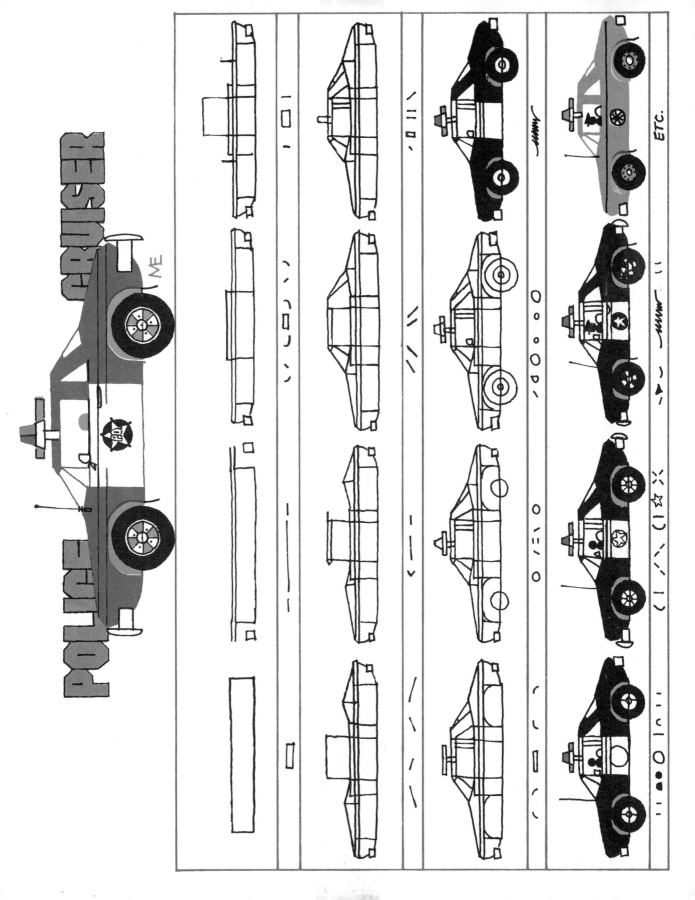

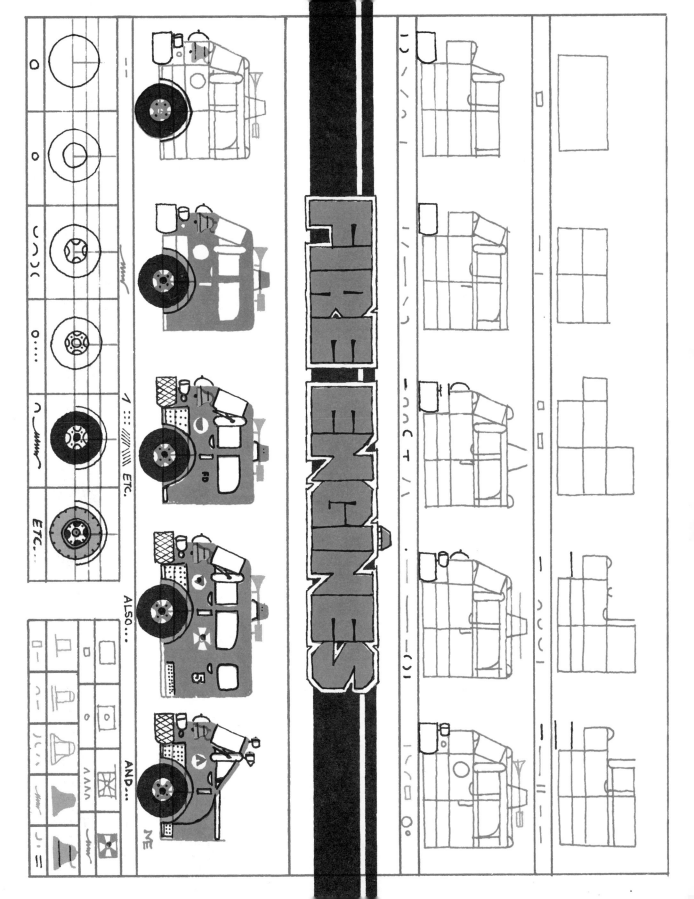

FIRE ENGINES

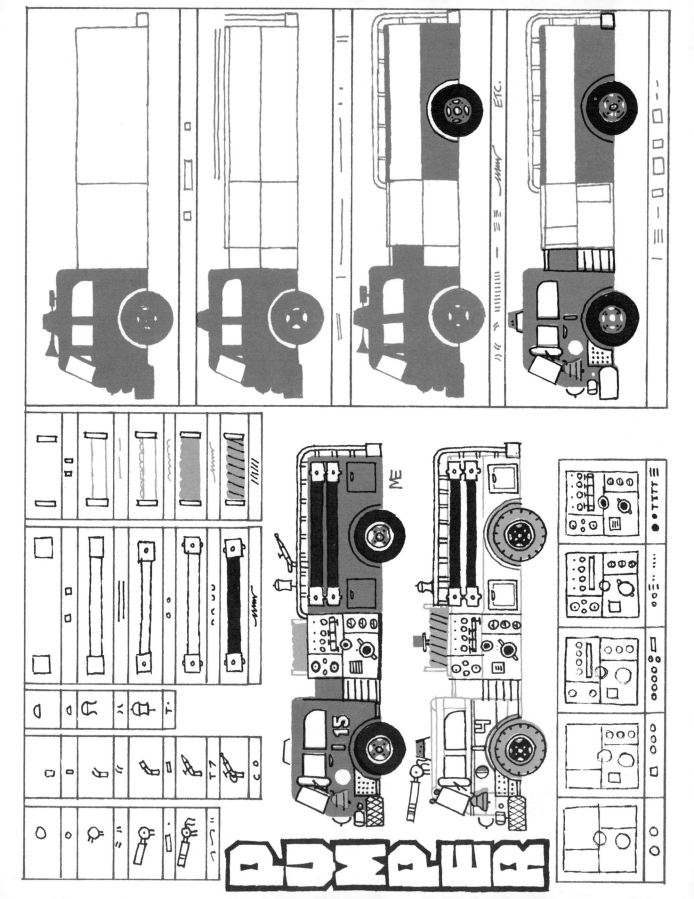

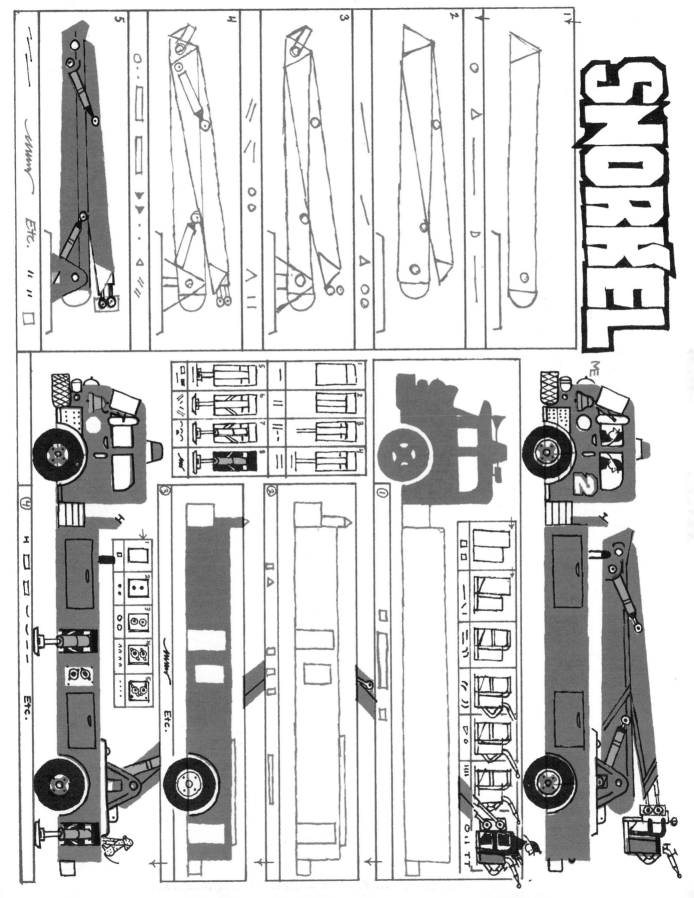

SNORKEL

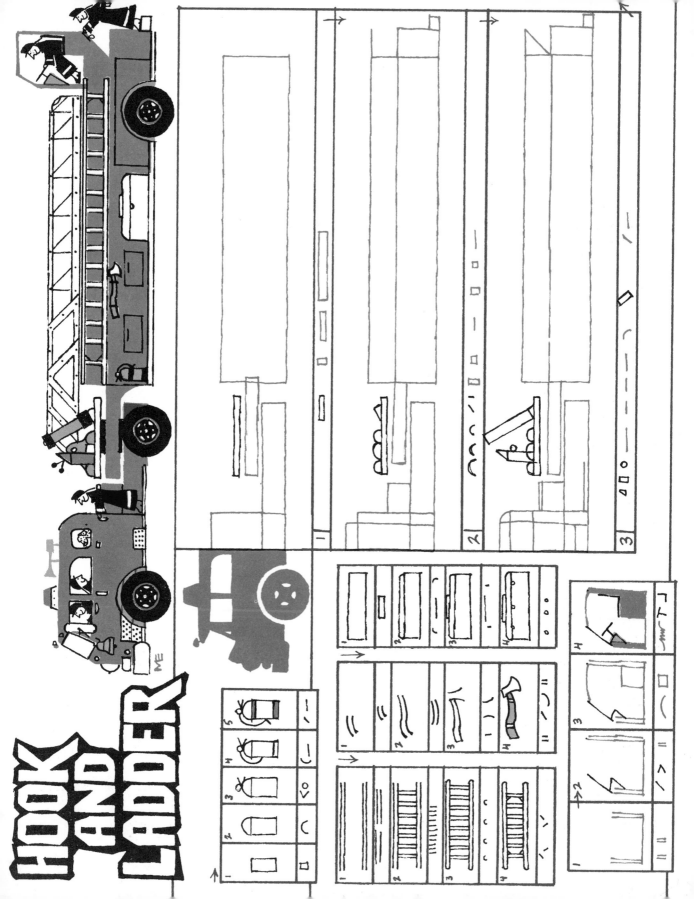

HOOK AND LADDER

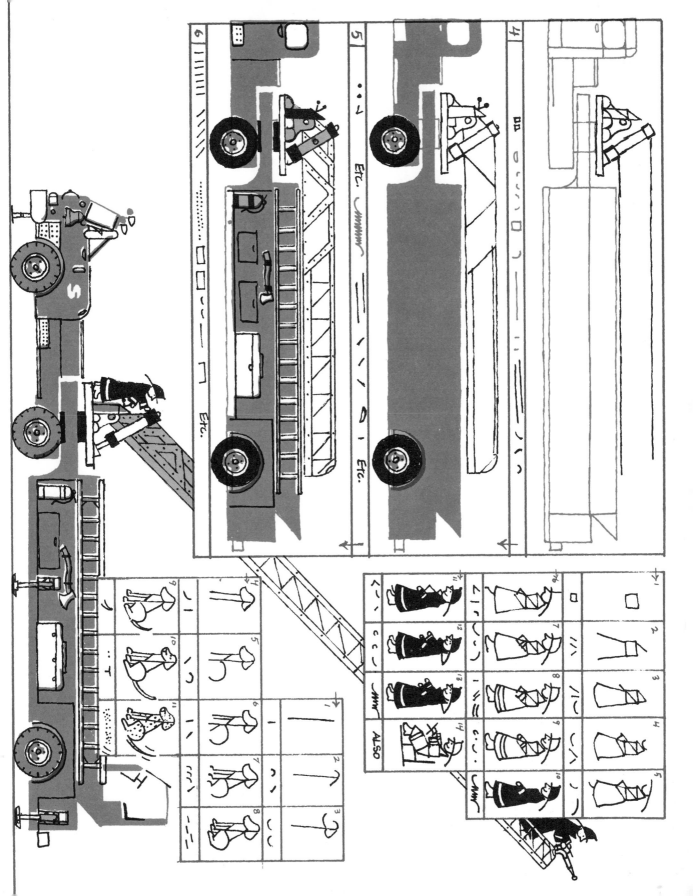

FEEDLE

FOODLE AS SEEN FROM F

EDLE SPACESHIP

(NICKNAME..."THE FEEDLE NEEDLE")

FEEDLE BIRDS

...SPARENT (AS ALL ELSE
FEEDLE) FEEDLE BIRDS FLY VERY WELL.

FOODLE

FOODLE AND FEEDLE ARE THE TWIN MOONS OF PLANET ZORT. (ZORT IN BIG GREEN DRAWING BOOK.)

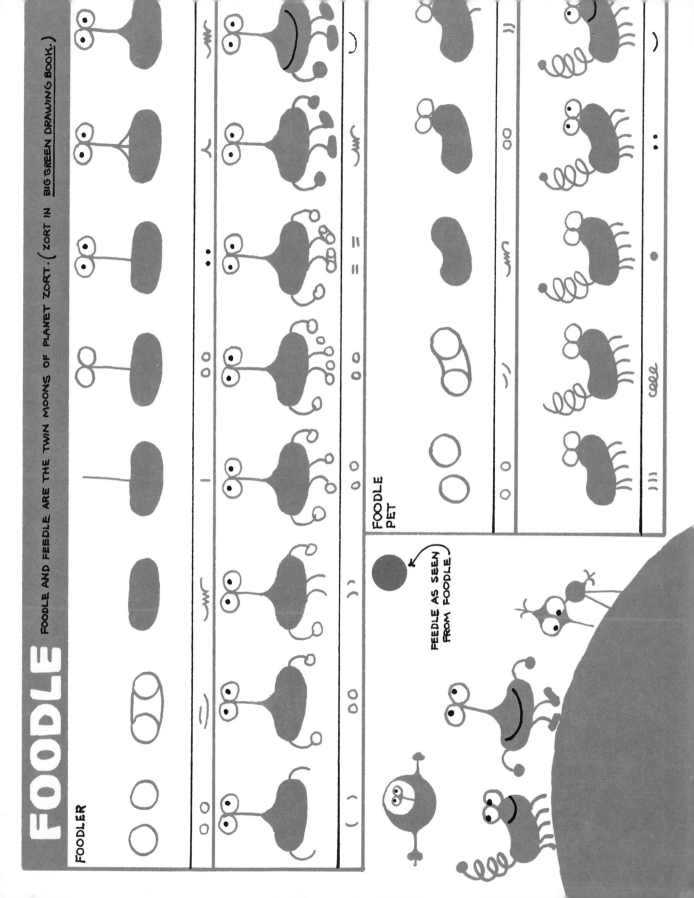

FOODLER

FOODLE PET

FEEDLE AS SEEN FROM FOODLE.

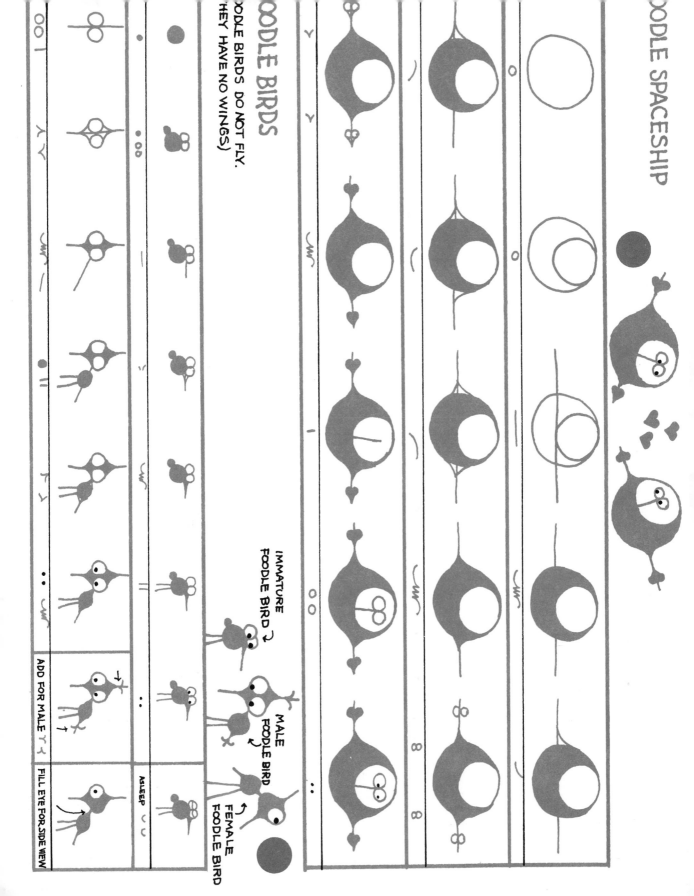

FOODLE SPACESHIP

FOODLE BIRDS

(FOODLE BIRDS DO NOT FLY.
THEY HAVE NO WINGS)

IMMATURE
FOODLE BIRD

MALE
FOODLE BIRD

FEMALE
FOODLE BIRD

ADD FOR MALE

FILL EYE FOR SIDE VIEW

ASLEEP

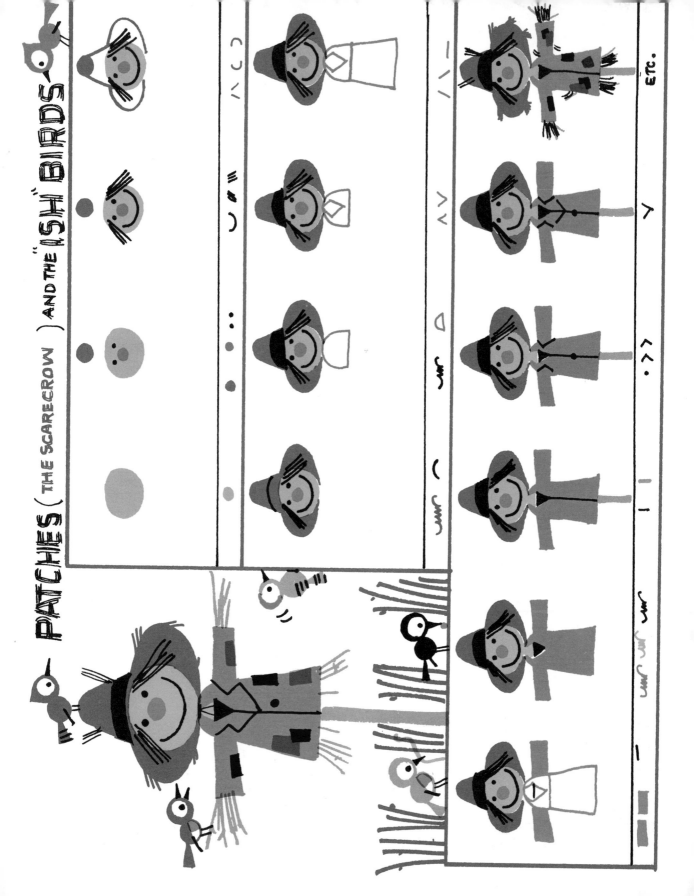

PATCHES (THE SCARECROW) AND THE "ISH" BIRDS

("ISH" BIRDS ARE SMALL IMAGINARY BIRDS
THAT REMIND YOU OF CERTAIN REAL BIRDS.)

BLUE BIRDISH
SORT OF A BIRD

JAYISH
SORT OF A BIRD

CARDINALISH
SORT OF A BIRD

ROBINISH
SORT OF A BIRD

CROWISH
SORT OF A BIRD

WOODPECKERISH
SORT OF A BIRD

JAY

JAYISH
BIRD

ROBINISH
BIRD

ROBIN

BROWN

TWO WAYS TO DRAW A PEANUT.

RUNNING

RABBITS!

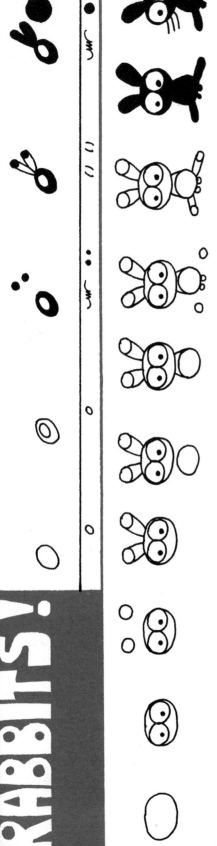

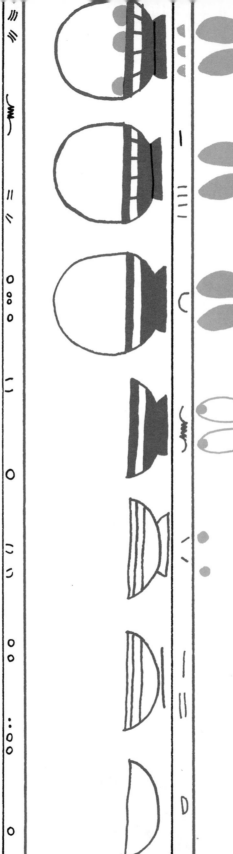

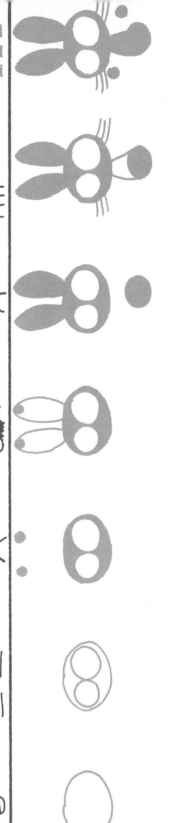